GOD LOVES ME TOO
31 DAY DEVOTIONAL

Janice Robinson

Copyright

Table of Contents

"I have loved you, my people, with an everlasting love. With unfailing love, I have drawn you to myself."

Jeremiah 31:3b NLT

Introduction

◆

The very first Bible verse I learned as a child was John 3:16 "For God so loved the world, that he gave his only begotten Son, that whosoever believeth in Him should not perish, but have everlasting life." I didn't have a revelation of what that scripture really meant until I got older. I knew God loved the world, that His Son Jesus died for our sins, but it wasn't personal to me. I had no revelation of how God could love me with all the things I'd done. Even though I was living in sin, He still loved me. I didn't understand nor did I realize His love covered my sin no matter how bad it was.

In our world today, there are so many people who don't know that God loves them unconditionally. So many are looking for love in relationships, but if we have not received the love God has for us, how can we love others? God longs for relationship with us all. We were created for the purpose of worshipping, loving, and fellowshipping with the Father. Until that relationship is on point, until we are complete in Him, we can't expect our relationship with others to be productive! "Yes, I am the vine; you are the branches. Those who remain in me, and I in them, will produce much fruit. For apart from me you can do nothing" (John 15:5 NLT).

Jesus is our true love, lover of our soul. "He is love, and all who live in love live in God, and God lives in them" (1 John 5:16). He's the one who completes us. He is the only one who can fill the emptiness we feel in our heart. That place was designed for Him and Him only. It is up to us to receive His love. His love for us will remain forever. As you read this devotional, I pray you will experience God's love for you. The experiences I share are just a few to let you know how God loved me through some rough times in my life. Just like He loves me, He loves you too! He is waiting with open arms to receive you. Receive His love today and begin the journey with Him!

Day 1

"I will give thanks and praise to You, for I am fearfully and wonderfully made" Psalms 139:14 (Amplified).

WHY DID GOD MAKE ME?

A student of mine once asked me this question years ago. She said, "Ms. Robinson!" I responded, "Yes!" Then she asked, "Why did God make me?" I looked at her with amazement. Just out of the blue, this kindergartener asked me such a profound question. I was speechless at first, wondering how I should respond. No one had ever asked me that question before. I don't recall asking myself that question. How was I going to be able to explain to her why God made her, and she understand? Then I told her, "Because He loves you, and you are special to him. Don't you ever forget it!"

Yes we are special to Him! God made us in his image and his likeness or to be like him (Genesis 1:26). We were created for His glory and to give him praise! There is nothing more important to God than when he created human beings. Not the animals, the fish in the sea, or any other creature is more important to him than humans. He loves us with an everlasting love (Jeremiah 31:3)!

Remember this, no matter what you've done in your life, good or bad, God will never stop loving you! When no one else loves you or cares about you,

God cares. When people talk about you or even try to bully you, remember you are loved by God!

Lord, I receive your love for me, I love myself and ask you to love on others through me. In Jesus' name, amen!

$\mathcal{D}$ay 2

GOD KNEW YOU WHEN

"For those whom He foreknew [and loved and chose beforehand], He also predestined to be conformed to the image of His Son [and ultimately share in His complete sanctification], so that He would be the firstborn [the most beloved and honored] among many believers" (Romans 8:29, AMP).

God knew you when you were living in sin. Whether you were having sex before marriage, an alcoholic, a drug user, a drug dealer, a prostitute, gambler, cheater, a thief, an adulterer, a liar, or murderer. Whatever your sin, God knew you before all that, yet He still loved you. He gave his life for YOU! He chose YOU to be a part of his kingdom. That's amazing! "For God so loved the world that He gave His only begotten son. That whosoever believeth in him should not perish but have everlasting life" (John 3:16). Guess what? You were on his mind when he hung on the cross. If you were the only one in this world, Jesus still would have given his life just for you! God knew you then, and he knows you now. He has an awesome plan for your life. Forget about your past and give God your life! Now take a moment and say this prayer.

Heavenly Father, I come to you now asking you to forgive me of my sin. I ask that you come into my heart, save me, baptize me, and fill me with the Holy Ghost. I receive your forgiveness by faith in your son Jesus' name. Amen!

Day 3

"Don't be dejected and sad, for the joy of the LORD is your strength" (Nehemiah 8:10 NLT).

LIVE! LOVE! LAUGH!

These three words have been seen on images, in magazines, on artwork, etc. I want to share a personal testimony with you. After my divorce, the Lord spoke to me one morning during my time of communion with Him. He said, "Daughter, I want you to have fun and enjoy life." He didn't say love this life; this world, but enjoy what I have put here for you to enjoy while you're here on this earth. John 10:10 says, "The thief cometh not, but for to steal, and to kill, and to destroy. I am come that they might have life and have it more abundantly."

The word abundantly when translated in the Greek means exceeding, going beyond; full, excessive. So what does this mean? It means God wants his people to live life to the fullest. Allow him to take you on an adventure. Be open to doing things you've never done before. Go places you've never gone before. As he leads by His spirit, don't be afraid to step out on faith and follow your dreams. God has put everything in you to help you be all He predestined you to be. Live your life knowing that God has your back! Love yourself and let God love on others through you. Don't let what's happening in the world around you get you depressed and sad! Learn to laugh! "A merry heart doeth good like a medicine: but a broke spirit drieth the bones" (Proverbs 17:22 KJV). You know the saying "It takes more muscles to frown than to smile." So smile people! Live! Love! Laugh!

Lord, I will live the life you have predestined me to live. I choose to not allow the enemy to steal my joy so that I won't be without your strength. I have a cheerful heart because that's what keeps me healthy. In Jesus' name! Amen!

Day 4

"But when the right time came, God sent his Son, born of a woman, subject to the law" (Galatians 4:4 NLT).

GOD'S TIMING!

One day, I was talking to a young lady from my former church about how God blessed me with a new car. I was so excited about how God did it that I had to share all the details with her. I told her that my old car had clonked out on me, and I was without a car for about a month. Then one Saturday the Lord spoke to me and said, "Go get your car!" I asked him, "Where should I go Lord?" He told me to go to Carmax. So, I said, "Lord, I thank you that I will be at the right place, at the right time, and purchase the car I want with the right salesperson to assist me." The Lord gave me exactly what I asked for.

After sharing that information with her, she said, "Did God really have to tell you to go get a car? You were without a car, so you shouldn't have to wait for God to tell you, just go get it!" Does that sound familiar? It sounds similar to what the serpent said to Eve in the garden. "Did God really say you must not eat the fruit from any trees in the garden?" (Genesis 3:1 NLT). I didn't say anything to the young lady for a minute, then I responded, "It was God's timing." He knew the right time for me to go get the car because He had already lined things up for me before the foundation of the world. Everything and everyone had to be at the right place at the right time in order for God's plan for me to manifest. Had I gone ahead and did things on my own, I would not have received God's best. I always wanted a Toyota Camry. God knew the timing was right, and I was in the right position to receive what he wanted to give me.

God's timing is so important! It can save us from a lot of trouble and most of all save our lives!

Lord Jesus, your timing is always perfect! Holy Spirit help me to not go on my own, but trust that everything you have planned for me is already done and will manifest at the right time. In Jesus' name, amen!

Day 5

"Choose you this day whom ye will serve?" "But as for me and my house we will serve the LORD" (Joshua 24:15).

CONSEQUENCES OR REWARD?

"Choosing rather to suffer affliction with the people of God, than to enjoy the pleasures of sin for a season" (Hebrews 11:25).

The Bible is clear when it says sin is pleasurable for a season, but afterwards comes death. When Adam ate the forbidden fruit in the Garden of Eden, the whole world was sentenced to death, but Jesus gave his life for the whole world and now we have a choice to live eternally with him. Romans 5:17 (NLT) states, "For the sin of this one man, Adam, caused death to rule over many. But even greater is God's wonderful grace and his gift of righteousness, for all who receive it will live in triumph over sin and death through this one man, Jesus Christ."

This wonderful grace and gift of righteousness is ours if we want it. We can choose to remain in sin and spend eternity in a burning hell, or we can choose to receive the gift of salvation and spend eternity with God. In first Peter 3:9 NLT, it states, "The Lord isn't really being slow about his promise, as some people think. No, he is being patient for your sake. He does not want anyone to be destroyed, but wants everyone to repent." We are living in a time of grace, and we don't know the day or hour in which Jesus will return.

Therefore, we must make a decision today about where we want to spend eternity. Do you want to receive the consequences of not receiving Jesus as Lord and Saviour, or do you want the reward which comes with receiving Jesus as Lord and Saviour? I would rather choose Jesus to be my Lord and not need him, than to not choose him and need Him! The choice is yours!

Lord, I believe that your son Jesus will return at the appointed time you have chosen. Knowing that, help me by your spirit to make good choices today. I want to live eternally with you, so the first choice I will make is choosing you as Lord and Savior. I believe in the Lord so that me and my family will be saved. In Jesus' name, amen!

Day 6

"He that dwelleth in the secret place of the Most-High shall abide under the shadow of the almighty" (Psalm 91:1).

ONE IN A MILLION

The lottery is played by millions of people across the country. Some people have spent hundreds of dollars to increase their chances of winning. They believe if they could just hit the jackpot and win millions of dollars, their troubles will be over. The chances of winning the lottery are slim because the odds of becoming a single winner is one in 175 million. That's a lot of people and one would have to play the lottery quite often and still may never win.

Not so with Jesus! There's no money to be spent in order to win in life with the Lord! He is a winner. Therefore, if you are in Christ then you are a winner! You don't have to spend your lifesavings to get a breakthrough in life. All you have to do is spend time with him. Spending time in His presence will help you to win in life. Spending time with Jesus will help you be successful each day because you're getting instructions from him to get you through the day.

Communing with the Father brings peace and joy; it brings security knowing that you are dwelling and abiding in the secret place of the Most-High God! There is no fear, worries, disappointments, anxieties, or trouble in His presence! With winning the lottery comes problems, trials, and tribulations because your focus is on money and material things, not on God. So, instead of taking your chances (one in 175 million) on playing the lottery and wasting money that could be put away in a savings for you, take your chances on Jesus and be a winner every time!

Lord, thank you that I have access to you anytime I want. I ask that you order my steps this day so that you will get the glory out of my life. I put my trust in you knowing that you will never leave nor abandon me. In Jesus' name, amen!

$\mathcal{D}$ay 7

"And God saw everything that he had made, and behold, it was very good" (Gen1:31a, AMP).

A MASTERPIECE

You are a masterpiece! You were created by a skilled artist, almighty God! When God created man, He put in him everything he needed to live on this earth. He took a rib from the man and made the woman. He (God) is detailed; he made the woman using the man's rib, but he made her with different parts so to distinguish her from the man. Her hair, curves, and special body parts are all unique. The interesting thing about Gods creation is that no one has the same finger prints. Out of over 6 billion people on planet Earth, not a single one of us has the same finger print. That's amazing!

After the fall of man, sin stained the masterpiece that God created. We were all born into sin because of what Adam did in the garden (Gen. 3:6-7). But God already had a plan in place. He sent His son Jesus to die for our sins so we could be born again! Ephesians 2:10 states, "For we are his workmanship, created in Christ Jesus unto good works, which God hath before ordained."

The word workmanship in the Greek is poiema, pronounced (poy'-ay mah). It means a creation, things that are made. So, we were made new in Christ when we received Him as Lord and Savior. Our lives were spiritually transformed. Workmanship in Webster's dictionary means the quality imparted to a thing in the process of making. When purchasing a brand-new Range Rover, the company doesn't just make these particular vehicles in the United States. They are made in the United Kingdom and made to the purchaser's specification. Whatever features you want in this vehicle is what the manufacturer will build. Then it is shipped to the dealership and delivered to the purchaser. The more you want the more you'll pay. These vehicles start at $85k.

Well, the same with us, God not only made our physical body, but He gave us a brain that controls motor functions and the ability to interpret information. He also deposited in us gifts and talents to be used for his glory. He paid the ultimate price for us. We are more valuable to him than anything in this world. As the song writer said, "God don't make no junk!" We are made in His image and after His likeness! We are His masterpiece!

Lord, you are the potter and I am the clay. Continue the good work you started in me, so that I will be made perfect upon your return. In Jesus' name, amen!

Day 8

"And the Word was made flesh and dwelt among us (and we beheld his glory, the glory as of the only begotten of the Father,) full of grace and truth" (John 1: 14).

FAIRY TALES

One of my favorite R&B artist is Anita Baker. I like her smooth, silky, sultry voice. She sings a song called Fairy Tales, and in the song, she talks about stories her mom read to her at night, you know them: **Cinderella, Snow White, and Sleeping Beauty,** just to name a few. These were the fairy tales we grew up on thinking that we would meet a handsome prince/princess, marry him/her and live happily ever after. Unfortunately, fairy tales don't always come true, and we have to deal with the realities of this world. There is good news though. There is hope because we have met the prince, Jesus. He is the Prince of Peace! He is our knight and shining armor, the word that became flesh, the one who was, and is and is to come. His spirit lives within us if we are born again believers. He is the one who never breaks our heart, leaves us for another man/woman, loves us conditionally, nor does He physically or verbally abuses us. He won't prostitute us, financially break us, or abandon us.

Christ can be trusted; he is dependable, faithful, loving, caring, and a true gentleman! He is our protector, provider, healer, lover, and strength. He is all that and much more! He has given his life for us! In Him is joy, peace of mind, and life eternal.

There is no make believe, magic potions, or spells to be broken. He has defeated the evil prince (Satan) and given us the power to keep the enemy at bay and one word from Him will change our lives forever! He is the **King of Kings** and **Lord of Lords**! He is Jesus the only begotten of the father and that **ain't** no **fairy tale**!

Father God, you are my everything! Without you I am nothing. You are the one true God and there is no other. You are the lover of my soul and that love will last forever. Thank you so much for loving me! In Jesus' name, amen!

Day 9

"If ye abide in me, and my words abide in you, ye shall ask what ye will, and it shall be done unto you" (John 15:7).

ABIDING IN LOVE

The Lord has been speaking to me more and more about trusting him no matter what circumstances I encounter. His words have been a constant reminder to me that He is in control and not me! When things happen, I try to figure out how I can fix it when the truth is God has already taken care of it!

In my former church, where I grew up, the choir sang a song titled "God Is." Basically, the message of the song is God is everything we need and want. He will never leave us. He is a God of his word. We can trust in him when we go through trials and hardships. When we're down to our last dime, we can trust God to be our provider. When things aren't going the way we want them to, God knows, and sees, and all we have to do is keep our mind on him, the "Word."

John 15:1 says, "I am the true vine." In other words, He is our life line, our life support; the one whom we can depend on. What is a tree without branches? What is a tree without roots? When we are connected to the vine, Jesus, we get his strength, his anointing, his power, and his protection. What a wonderful feeling it is to be loved by God, to know that he can be trusted, and we can depend on Him! I don't know about you, but I can't be disconnected from the "True Vine!" Why don't you get connected today?

Lord, you are my life, without you I can't live. I disconnect myself from everything that is non-productive in my life and I stay connected to you the true vine. Amen!

Day 10

"For He hath made him to be sin for us, who knew no sin, that we might be made the righteousness of God in him" (2 Corinthians 5:21).

RIGHTEOUSNESS, IT'S YOURS!

In June of 2000, I relocated to Georgia. I lived in a suburb 20 miles north of Atlanta and attended a church in College Park. I can remember attending Sunday morning service and Bible Study on Wednesday nights. One night during Bible study, my pastor was teaching on righteousness. He kept repeating these words, "You are the righteousness of God. You were made righteous through the blood that Jesus shed on the cross of Calvary. You don't have to listen to what the devil says about you! You tell him you were made righteous through Jesus!" As I kept hearing the words, something began to happen! "Faith comes by hearing, and hearing, and hearing." The light bulb came on, and I began to see a little clearer. I realized that night I didn't have to fornicate anymore! I did not have to allow what others thought of me to determine what I should do, how I should live, or the choices I made. No more of the devil telling me that I could not have God's best because of what I'd done in the past, sins I committed, things that only me and God knew about. No more devil! No more!

When I received Jesus, he took away my sins and placed them as far as the east is from the west, never to remember them anymore. So, when the devil brings up my past, I tell him it's under the blood.

The same for you, my friends, when you received Jesus as Lord and Savior, he made you righteous! He took our unrighteousness (our sin) and gave us righteousness (eternal life, right standing with God the Father). It's like we never sinned because Jesus dealt with our sins on the cross and said, "It is finished!"

So when the devil tries to remind you of your past, you tell him it's under the blood of Jesus! Jesus made me righteous!

This message was approved and paid for by Jesus and the blood he shed on Calvary!

Lord Jesus, thank you for the blood you shed on cavalry that put me in right standing with the Father. I cancel every attack in my mind from the enemy that tries to keep me bound and prevent me from moving ahead. I'm forgetting those things that are behind me, and I look forward to the bright future you have planned for me. In Jesus' name, amen!

$\mathcal{D}$ay 11

"If someone says, "I love God," but hates a Christian brother or sister, that person is a liar; for if we don't love people we can see, how can we love God, whom we cannot see?" 1John 4:20 (NLT).

LOVE DOESN'T HURT!

1 Corinthians 13:4-7 is part of my daily confession along with Romans 5:5 NLT "And this hope will not lead to disappointment. For we know how dearly God loves us because he has given us the Holy Spirit to fill our hearts with love. The love the writer Paul is referring to is unconditional love that will last forever, a pure love that comes from almighty God. We experience that love when we have fellowship/relationship with the father.

This is the same kind of love the Lord wants us to have for each other, unconditional. Yet, in many relationships today this is not the case. In March 2014, my husband and I separated. I had been praying and believing God for things to turn around in our marriage and it didn't. After moving out, I asked my husband if we could start all over again, but he wasn't willing to do that. I continued to pray and ask the Lord to save my marriage and move by his spirit on my husband's heart. One morning, the Lord spoke to me and said these words, "It's time for you to move on with your life because he (my husband) is not willing to change."

Was I ready to move on? No, however, I had to. If a person is not willing to change, then it's time to let go. Now, hear me. I'm not saying you should leave your spouse! Every situation, be it the same, will have different results. You must seek the Lord regarding your marriage and do only what He tells you to do! God made sure that he prepared me to leave the situation to protect both he and I. There was no physical abuse involved, only emotional, and that's just as bad. You may be in an abusive relationship and feel trapped. I urge you to seek God's guidance and spiritual counsel from your pastor or a minister you trust who will pray with you and for you regarding your situation. If there are children from the marriage, you want to do what's right to protect them, too. There are many abuse hotline numbers you can call, and they can help you find a safe place if your situation requires that. God does not intend for people to be abused. When people don't know the proper use for something, they will ab-use it! Unless the abuser gets some professional help, do not go back merely because they said, "I'm sorry." They need professional help because they will repeat the behavior if they are not willing to change.

When someone truly loves you, they won't cause you any harm. I know things happen in a relationship such as arguments and disagreements, but love does not **purposely** hurt. Love's intentions are to bring peace in times of difficulties. It is to agree to disagree and come to a quick resolution where both parties are satisfied with the outcome. To love means to protect, provide, take the blame, encourage, share, and respect. Ephesians 5:25 says this to husbands, "Husbands, love your wives, even as Christ also loved the church and gave himself for it." So, how does Christ love the church? He protects us and provides for us. He took the blame by carrying our sin, sickness, and disease in his body and dealt with it on the cross. He sent the Holy Ghost to encourage, uplift, and remind us of his love. He shares with us. What's his is ours! Lastly, he respects us to the point that if we decided we don't want him in our life, he will not violate our will, because He is a gentlemen! That's love, and that kind of love doesn't hurt!

Lord, you are my healer, the mender of broken hearts. Where there is hurt bring healing. Where there is disappointment, bring happiness and satisfaction. Where there is confusion, bring peace and order. Restore the joy of your salvation in my heart and help me to obey you! I am complete in you alone! In Jesus' name, amen!

$\mathcal{D}$ay 12

"Greater love hath no man than this that a man lay down his life for his friends" (John 15: 13, KJV)

LOVE IS.....

When I was a little girl, I can remember the Chicago newspapers being delivered to our house. One newspaper I love to read was the Chicago Tribune---yes, I read the paper when I was little. There was a comic strip titled "Love Is." This comic strip was the result of a young woman who had written love notes to her future husband. These love notes were interesting and heartwarming. My sister and I would cut them out and tape them in the mirror. This four letter word **l o v e** is an action word and sometimes it is used lightly. Men and women have said, "I love you," in a way to get what they want.

So what is true love? True love from the Lord is amazing. It is unconceivable. "And may you have the power to understand, as all God's people should, how wide, how long, how high and how deep his love is." Ephesians 3:18 (NLT). **He** (God/Jesus)is our true love. "And we have known and believed the love that God hath toward us. God is love; and he that dwelleth in love dwelleth in God, and God in Him."

Love is knowing that we cannot be separated from His love. "For I am persuaded that neither death, nor life, nor angels, nor principalities, nor powers, nor things present, nor things to come. Nor height, nor death, nor any other creature, shall be able to separate us from the love of God, which is in Christ Jesus our Lord" Romans 8:38-39 (KJV). That's what love is!

Lord, you are love! Your love is so deep that I can't comprehend. The love you have placed in heart is not proud, boastful, arrogant, jealous, or rude. It is not self-seeking or impatient but a genuine love like yours! I will not allow anything to separate me from your love. In the name of Jesus'! Amen!

$\mathcal{D}$ay 13

"Stay alert! Watch out for your enemy, the devil. He prowls around like a roaring lion, looking for someone to devour" (1Peter 5:8, NLT).

THE DETRACTOR IS A DISTRACTION

I have been single for a few years now and thought I was ready to start dating again. I met this gentlemen at the car dealership where I take my car to be serviced. He had asked me several times if he could take me out to lunch or dinner. After a few times of him asking me out, I finally said yes. He called me and set up a day, time and place for us to meet. Well, on my way to our meeting place, I sensed in my spirit that he wouldn't show up. I got there and he was not there. I texted him and called him but he did not respond to neither my text nor phone call. So, I went home. I wasn't mad or upset that he stood me up, no, as a matter of fact I was glad!

The next morning during my time of prayer I asked the Lord "What was that all about?" The Lord said to me, "He is a detractor and a distraction!" I thought a detractor?! What does that mean? **Detractor**, a person who disparages someone or something. In other words, a person who devalues another, belittles, slanders, or a denigrator. Wow! I have been with a few of those kind of men. I don't need or want that anymore and neither do YOU! We need to know that we are valuable and should not let anyone bring us down. We don't need any distractions because that's what the enemy uses to keep us from receiving God's best for us. Ladies, if you are believing God for a husband, and men if you're believing God for a wife, then wait on Him to bring you together. He is the ultimate matchmaker. He knows what we need, and he will bring us his best. He always does! Jesus is the best gift that God has given to the world. He loved the world so much that he gave his only begotten son! He loves and values us so much so that we should love and value ourselves. Keep away from the **detractor,** and don't allow any **distractions** to keep you from receiving what God has for you!

Lord, I know that you love me and want what's best for me. I will not manipulate events by letting my flesh get in the way but will wait patiently on you. In Jesus' name, amen!

Day 14

"But if anyone does sin, we have an advocate who pleads our case before the Father. He is Jesus Christ, the one who is truly righteous. He himself is the sacrifice that atones for our sins- and not only our sins but the sins of the world" 1John 2:1b &2 (NLT)

THERE IS NO CONDEMNATION

One day at work, I spoke to a little girl; let's just say her name was April, and asked how she was doing?

She said, "Oh, I'm bad! I'm just bad."

I replied, "April, you're not bad!"

She continued, "Oh yes I am! There is nothing good about me."

Then, I asked, "Sweetheart, who told you that?

She said, "Nobody! I just know I'm bad!"

I thought about what she said. She was referring to her behavior, and she was right because we were all born in sin. That's why we have to be born again! There is no good thing in us. "Wherefore, as one man sin entered into the world and death by sin, and so death passed upon all men, for that all have sinned." Romans 5:12 (KJV). Before Adam sinned, he knew no evil, but after his fall, he knew good and evil. But God, sent his son Jesus, and he died to save humanity from our sin. "But there is a great difference between Adam's sin and

God's gracious gift. For the sin of this one man, Adam, brought death to many. But even greater is God's wonderful grace and his gift of forgiveness to many through this other man, Jesus Christ" (Romans 5:15, NLT).

Unfortunately, too many of us think that we are so bad that we can't be used by God. The Devil/Satan, who is our enemy, attacks our mind with thoughts that we are bad and not good enough. Therefore, we can't be used by God. He is a liar and the father of lies. His job is to try and keep us from knowing the truth and that is that God loves us regardless of what we may have done or how many times we messed up and feel like a failure. The Lord is not condemning us nor is he pointing His finger at us because we missed the mark. Satan goes before the Father day and night accusing us because of our wrong doing, but when we sin, we have an advocate, Jesus, who is forever interceding for us and pleading our case before the father saying, "Not Guilty!" Does this give us a license to sin? No, of course not, but when we sin, we can go to the Father through Jesus and ask for forgiveness, and He is faithful to forgive us and cleanse us of all unrighteousness."

So, the next time Satan tries to bring thoughts of condemnation or guilt, you tell him "There is therefore now no condemnation to them which are in Christ Jesus, who walk not after the flesh, but after the spirit."

Lord, thank you that my life is hid in you. I am righteous because of the blood of Jesus. When I miss the mark, you are not condemning me (bringing guilt or shame) but only grace and mercy. When Satan tries to make me feel guilty, I say to him, "I am forgiven and you are defeated in Jesus' name, amen!"

Day 15

"Charm is deceptive, and beauty does not last; but a woman who fears the LORD will be greatly praised" (Proverbs 31:30, NLT).

BEAUTY'S ONLY SKIN DEEP!

Ladies! Ladies! Ladies! We spend hundreds of dollars on beauty products to keep ourselves looking beautiful. As we mature, we spend even more money on products to prevent signs of aging. Why? Is it so we can look good for ourselves or others? Do we spend more time working on the outward appearance or the inward? I've had to ask myself this same question. For years, I thought I was too fat, not cute enough, not good enough, not smart enough; all those thoughts that the enemy, Satan, attacked my mind with, and I'm sure I'm not alone.

One thing I've learned is this, how we look on the outside, is less important than how we look on the inside. 1Peter 3:4 (KJV) says, "But let it be the hidden man of the heart, in that which is not corruptible, even the ornament of a meek and quiet spirit, which is in the sight of God of great price." What is Peter talking about? He's talking about cultivating the inner beauty. A woman with a quiet gentle spirit, one who displays godly character can get the attention of her husband who may not be a believer. How does she carry herself around others when the two are out in public? Is she telling him off, cursing him out or totally disrespecting him in public and in private? This message from Peter is not just for married women but women in general.

I attended an event some time ago. It required me to dress in a formal evening gown or cocktail dress. I went alone and because the hotel parking lot was full, I had to park three blocks away and walk back to the hotel. I wore a red off the shoulder dress with red heels and silver accessories. Yes, I was looking good and the weather was perfect for the end of March! While walking to the hotel I received compliments from several well dressed, good looking men. After the event, I headed back to my car. It was a beautiful night for walking. There were a lot of people out enjoying the warm breeze of the night air. I stopped at the traffic light so I could cross the street. While I was waiting, about 5 or 6 men were walking behind me and I heard a few whistling and saying, "Lady in red, lady in red! Baby you look good in that red!" I responded by saying, "Good evening gentlemen! Thank you!" One gentlemen even stopped to take a look at me from the front and asked, "Do you have a date tonight, Baby?" I smiled and said, "Yes, I do!" Then I said, "You gentlemen enjoy your evening!"

Now, I said this to say some time ago I would not have been so nice. I would have had an attitude and got smart with them and said some mean things. They didn't mean any harm, but it was all in my response. Had I said the mean things they probably would have said some mean things to me. For one, even though these men saw beauty on the outside, my response, my attitude and smile were a reflection of what's on the inside. Two, had I responded in an ugly manner, making them think they were beneath me, I would have blown my witness. Did this happen overnight? No, it is a process and takes us continually going before the father and asking him to help us by his spirit to be the God fearing, kind, gentle, loving person he has called us to be. The word of God tells us, "Love is patient. Love is kind; it is not rude. It is not provoked [nor overly sensitive and easily angered]" (1Corinthians 13:4-5, AMP). There is an old saying, "You catch more with honey than with vinegar."

Lord, help me by your spirit to be sweet like you. I will use your word and speak over my life, working from the inside out so that when others see me, they see you! In Jesus' name, amen!

$\mathcal{D}$ay 16

"And Solomon, my son, learn to know the God of your ancestors intimately. Worship and serve him with your whole heart and a willing mind. For the LORD sees every heart and knows every plan and thought. If you seek him, you will find him. But if you forsake him, he will reject you forever" (1 Chronicles 28:9, NLT).

"I'M IN A RELATIONSHIP!"

How often have you heard the line, "I'm in a relationship?" R & B artist Erykah Badu sings a song titled "Next Lifetime." You may be familiar with it, but if not, the song starts out with a conversation between her and a male friend who wants more than a friendship. He wants to be her man. She really likes him too and tells him she's in a relationship. She says, "Now what am I supposed to do when I want you in my world, but how can I want you for myself when I'm already someone's girl." I thought about those words "I'm in a relationship" and asked myself what does it mean when a person says there in a relationship? I know there are different types of relationships (i.e familia, marriage, friends, etc.), but what about a relationship between a single man and female? What does this mean? So, I posed this question to my friends on social media and asked them to share what it means to them. I got some interesting responses. Some of my more mature friends, and some of my younger friends had good dialogue about this statement. There were two consistent words from all those who responded. They were **commitment** and **quality time.**

Even though I'm not married now nor dating anyone, I'm in a relationship! I'm in a relationship with God/Jesus. He is everything to me! I'm in love with him, and He's in love with me. We're **committed** to each other and we spend **quality time** with one another! He's all I need! I have learned that this relationship I have with the Father is far more important than any other and if this relationship doesn't work neither will any other. Psalm 91:1 says, "He that dwelleth in the secret place of the Most High shall abide under the shadow of the Almighty." There was a billboard that the Cook County Sheriff in Chicago posted some years ago. It said, "If you don't spend time with your children, they will spend time with us!" So, I say, when you spend time with the Father, it will be time well spent!

Lord, my relationship with you is more important than any other relationship. I choose to spend time with you each day so that I can build an intimate relationship with you and get to know you better. Amen!

Day 17

"While we look not at the things which are seen, but at the things which are not seen: for the things which are seen are temporal; but the things which are not seen are eternal" (2Corinthians 4:18).

ALL EYES ON ME!

When I want to get the attention of my students I say, "All eyes on me!" They respond by saying, "All eyes on you!" I do this to get them to focus on what we're going to do next. It usually works the first time, but there are times when I have to repeat what I said to get the attention of some who may still be distracted.

I can hear the Lord saying to his people, "All eyes on me!" We are distracted by the things that are going on in the world. The news channels reporting about the world and chaos happening in our cities and neighborhoods are depressing. Day after day we see the turmoil and confusion in our government, and it has gripped the minds and hearts of God's people. We are distracted by the situations and crisis that come in our lives. Children being rebellious and disobedient, husbands and wives arguing and fighting, financial problems occurring, sickness affecting the body. What has happened is we have taken our eyes off the word of God.

In Acts 3:1-6 (KJV) Peter and John were in the temple during the hour of prayer. A lame man was laid at the gate of the temple and would ask for money as the people entered the temple. He sees Peter and John and asked them for money. Peter looks at the man and says to him, "Look on us." The man looked at them expecting to receive something from them. Then Peter said, "Silver and gold have I none, but such as I have give I thee: In the name of Jesus Christ of Nazareth rise up and walk." The word goes on to say that Peter took the man by his hands and lifted him up and "Immediately his feet and ankle bones received strength." The lame man was healed and began walking, and praising God. The point I want to make is that Peter and James had the spirit of God living on the inside of them and the anointing of God on their lives to speak to that situation and it had to change. They told him to look at them. In other words, they were telling him to look at the one on the inside of me that can change your situation. We have to make a conscious decision every day to look at Jesus, look at the word, keep our eyes on the Lord and not on our circumstances! Looking at our circumstances only magnify them and shrinks our faith and our God. Looking at the Word/Jesus shrinks our problems and magnifies the Lord! "O magnify the LORD with me, and let us exalt his name together." All eyes on Jesus!

Lord, I will look away from everything that is a distraction and keep my eyes focused on You. You are the one who will bring my faith to maturity. In Jesus' name, amen!

Day 18

"I have been young, and now am old; yet have I not seen the righteous forsaken, nor his seed begging for bread" (Psalm 37:25).

God Never Fails

God Never Fails is a song the choir sang at the church where I grew up. The chorus to the song goes like this: "God never fails, God never fails! He abides with me He gives me victory, God never fails! Just keep the faith and never cease to pray. Just walk upright morning, noon day and night, He'll be there. There's no need to worry, for God never fails."

This song is so true! God never fails! In February of 2016, my mother came to live with me. She was having some physical and mental challenges and said she wanted to be with me. The Lord had taken me off my job the year before in May of 2015. He had spoken to me and said, "I'm putting you in full time ministry. You won't lose anything and nothing is going out." I wasn't sure what he meant at the time about full time ministry until my mother called me to come get her from Chicago. It then became clear to me what the Lord had assigned for me to do. I couldn't leave my mom by herself because of her challenges, so, I had to live off my savings until it ran out. There I was with no job or income, taking care of my mother, and not able to pay my bills. I had a car note, insurance, mortgage, and utilities. Oh, and let's not forget groceries for two people. Well, during that time, I had to depend on Him daily for our needs.

I can recall the bill collectors calling me every day at the same time and sometimes twice a day. My house was about to be foreclosed on and my car repossessed. I would talk to the Lord and remind Him of what he said, "You won't lose anything and nothing is going out." I remember one morning during my prayer time, I told the Lord that the mortgage company is threatening to take my house! "What do you want me to do?" The Holy Ghost said, "This house belongs to the Lord, and because it belongs to me, no one can take it from you!" Then the spirit of the Lord brought this song to my remembrance, God Never Fails! He also said that things would be tight, but everything will happen on time! Well, let me tell you God is true to His word! The day before my mortgage was "supposed" to be sold on the courthouse steps, I received a call from the mortgage company that I had been approved for a loan modification, and my payment would be reduced to half the amount. God didn't stop there. He told me to give my car back to the finance company and He said, I have a surprise for you!"

What a surprise, the Lord bought me a brand-new car! God is so faithful! My lights, gas, and water were not shut off during that time. When the refrigerator was empty, God would see to it that we had food to eat! He is Jehovah-Jireh the God who sees and provides! He took care of me and my mom! When God tells you to take a step of faith, just do it and know that He will take care of you. You may experience some hard times, but if you would put your trust in almighty God, He will never fail you! He is no respecter of person. Because you belong to him he is obligated to take care of you! God Never Fails!

Lord, you are my provider, source, resource, and sustainer. Your word is true and everything contrary to it is a lie. I will not fear but trust You in every situation and circumstance that comes my way. You are faithful to what you promised! Amen!

$\mathcal{D}$ay 19

"For this is the will of God, even your sanctification, that ye should abstain from fornication: That every one of you should know how to possess his vessel in sanctification and honour" (1Thessalonians 4:3-4).

WE BELONG TO THE LORD!

Everything we have belongs to God! Our body belongs to the Lord. Yes, that's right, our body! "Don't you realize that your body is the temple of the Holy Spirit, who lives in you and was given to you by God? You don't belong to yourself, for God bought you with a high price. So, you must honor God with your body" 1Corinthians 6:19-20 (NLT).

Since we belong to the Lord we are to take care of His temple. We are to get the rest we need each night, eat right, exercise, and honor the spirit of God who lives in us. We should also be mindful of what we do with our body.

When I was younger, I was involved in different relationships with men whom I was not married to. When I say involved, I mean intimately. In other words I was fornicating. I remember some years later seeing an advertisement about safe sex. Safe sex is not having sex until you are married. The picture showed a naked man in the bed with naked women on both sides of him. The message was clear. When you are having sex with someone, they're giving you a piece of everyone else they've had sex with before you. Wow! Just think all the bodily fluid from your "partner" all the attitudes, anger, infection, hatred, and more are now mixed up with your bodily fluid. Not only that, your souls

44

are spiritually connected which result in ungodly soul ties. Then once you decide to get married, you have all these other people you slept with in the marriage bed with you and your spouse. God never intended for us to be sexually active before marriage. He ordained sex for marriage! "Marriage is honourable in all, and the bed undefiled, but whoremongers and adulterers God will judge" (Hebrew 13:4).

You might say, well things are different now. People are living together before marriage and having sex with each other, even Christians! Yep! This is true these things are happening even with Christians, but God never changes. His word will remain the same. "Jesus Christ, the same yesterday, and today, and forever." When we received Christ as Lord and savior, we made a decision to live for him. Does that mean we won't mess up? No! It means we don't practice sinning. We don't make it a habit to sin. We have the Holy Spirit living on the inside of us to help us, but when we sin, we have an advocate, Jesus Christ the sacrificial lamb. The world may be doing things that are contrary to the word of God, but we don't let the world influence us. If you are having a tough time abstaining from sex before marriage, ask the Holy Spirit to help you to honor God with your body. Ask him to take away the desire for sex until you get married. He will do that for you! How do I know? He did it for me, and He wants to help us be the godly men and women He has called us to be. We are to live our lives by the word of God! Jesus paid the price to save the whole world from sin and keep us from going to hell. It cost him His life!

Lord, thank you for the sacrifice you made for me so that I could be free from bondage of sin. I choose to live a life that pleases you. I choose to honor you with my life by abstaining from those things that grieve you and bring reproach and shame to your name. In the name of Jesus, amen!

Day 20

"For verily I say unto you, That whosoever shall say unto this mountain, be thou removed, and be thou cast into the sea; and shall not doubt in his heart, but shall believe that those things which he saith shall come to pass; he shall have whatsoever he saith" (Mark 11:23).

Speak the Word Only

Isaiah 55:10-11 (NLT) says, "The rain and snow come down from the heavens and stay on the ground to water the earth, producing seed for the farmer and bread for the hungry. It is the same with my word. I send it out, and it always produces fruit. It will accomplish all I want it to and prosper everywhere I send it." As I read this scripture one morning, I thought about the time I purchased my first home. I prayed and asked the Lord for a house in a nice community in Covington, Georgia. I did not want to have to do my own lawn, so in my asking I included that the lawn care would be provided. After asking the Lord, I thanked him every day for what he had already done before the foundation of the world. God not only gave me what I asked for, but He did above and beyond that! He is so awesome!

One year later, after purchasing my house, I noticed one of my bushes began to die. I had a total of four, and the other three were full and thick while the one looked bare. The Holy Spirit reminded me of the word I learned from my former pastor, which was I could speak the word of God to any situation, and it can change. So, the Lord told me to go get some miracle grow sprinkle

46

it on the bush and speak to it and command it to grow thick and full like the others. I did just what He said. Within a few weeks, I started seeing my bush grow back. I kept thanking God that it was full and thick, and I expected it to grow! Now, if I can speak the word over a bush and it grow, what about speaking the word on other matters in my life?

In Luke 7, Jesus was asked if He would come and heal a Centurion's servant who was sick and near death. So, Jesus went, but before he arrived at the officer's house, he was met by the officer's friends and told he didn't need to come to the house but to speak the word from where he was, and his servant would be healed. Jesus was so amazed at this man's faith and said he had not seen any faith like that "in all Israel!" Jesus is looking for this kind of faith from his people. If we would believe when we speak the word on a situation or circumstance, it would change, we would be doing what the word tells us to do! The world would see the word of God at work on this earth. Just because something looks bad to the natural eye doesn't mean it's dead in the spirit realm. We can speak life to a dead situation and watch it come back to life, just like I did with the bush! "Death and life are in the power of the tongue, and they that love it shall eat the fruit thereof." Jesus called Lazarus to come forth after being in the grave four days, and He came forth alive! The work that Jesus did we will do also and greater works will we do because Jesus has gone back to the Father. Today, you choose whether you will speak life or death to a problem in your life or your family's life! I choose to speak the word; it always brings good results!

Lord, each day I choose to speak your word over my life. I will say what your word says about my health, my family, and my finances. I will use your word to refute anything the enemy says about me and my family. I expect to see your word manifest in my life. In Jesus' name, amen!

$\mathcal{D}$ay 21

"I will bless the Lord at all times: his praise shall continually be in my mouth" (Psalm 34:1).

I WON'T COMPLAIN!

A friend of mine called me one day and said, "You have a lot to be thankful for! You are blessed with two wonderful sons who have not given you any major problems! They are fine young men raising and taking care of their families." She is absolutely right! I do have a lot to be thankful for and yes I am blessed with two awesome sons. When I was younger, I would always say I wanted four children two boys and two girls. Well, that was not God's plan for me, and I remember saying over and over again how much I wanted a daughter. One day I asked God, "Why did you give me two sons and not one son and one daughter?" The Lord simply said, "I gave you what you needed." He most certainly did give me what I needed, and they are such a blessing to me.

Sometimes, if we're not careful, we may begin complaining about things that didn't go as we had hoped or planned. God doesn't want us complaining about anything, not even a broken or cracked fingernail. He knows what's best for us! The children of Israel complained about not having any food to eat in the wilderness. They told Moses they had plenty of food to eat in Egypt, but he had brought them in the wilderness to starve to death (Exodus 16:1-3). They did not realize when they were complaining to Moses, they were actually complaining to the Lord. It was the Lord that led them to the wilderness, and he had already made provisions for them to eat. He gave them enough food for each household. No family had too little or too much! When we are faced with a difficulty in our lives, we must not complain, but thank God for the breakthrough. Thank God for how he has already provided for you. Thank the Lord for how he has already made a way of escape for you. Thank him for the victory! God's plans for you are good and not evil, to give you hope and a bright future! So, the next time you think about complaining, turn those negative thoughts into positives with the word of God. "For the mouth speaks what the heart is full of." Complaining won't give you a breakthrough but praise will. Praise your way to victory!

Lord, forgive me for murmuring or complaining about anything. I will bless you every chance I get and constantly speak your praises. Amen!

$\mathcal{D}$ay 22

"All glory to God forever and ever! Amen" (Galatians 1:5, NLT).

GIVE GOD THE GLORY!

I moved here to Atlanta from Chicago in June of 2000. I was a Chicago Public school teacher and made a decent salary. After arriving here in Atlanta, I started interviewing with several counties in Atlanta for a teaching position. I was so excited about the move that I didn't research the salary or benefits each county had to offer. I know now, if I had, I probably would have stayed in Chicago. I was offered a job in the county in which I was living and was told my starting salary would be $29,000 a year. $29,000 a year?! You got to be kidding me! On top of that, I would get paid monthly, in Chicago I was accustomed to getting paid bi-weekly. Seriously, I was ready to go back to Chicago! No way, was I going to settle for making that kind of money. It was a salary decrease for me of $21,000! Yes, that's right $21,000! So, one day I was talking to the Lord, and I said God what am I going to do with $29,000 a year, and how am I going to pay my expenses getting paid monthly instead of bi-weekly? Lord, how will I manage this? This is what I heard, "You moved to a new city with $200.00, a family, and a broken-down car, but I was faithful!"

The Lord reminded me of the testimony my former pastor gave during a Sunday morning service in 1995. When I heard his voice and those words he spoke, the Lord was letting me know all I had to do was trust and depend on him. He was my source and still is to this day! Well, let me tell you, God is a God of his word! He is Jehovah-Jireh, the Lord who provides! During the first year while living in Georgia, God paid off my car, my student loan, and I got an increase in my salary. I received an unexpected check in the mail from my previous employer, and in November of 2001, the Lord blessed me with purchasing a new home! Wow! It was like every time I looked around God had done something that left me in awe! It was happening so quick, and it was unexpected. That's just like our God to do the unexpected! He did that because He is so awesome and faithful to what he promised in his word. He kept reminding me he was with me, and he was taking care of me! He took care of me with the little that I had. I didn't stop paying my tithes or giving offerings. Sometimes, I didn't have much to eat or enough money for gas but God! All I can say is to God be the glory! As the Lord blesses you, don't forget to give him the glory!

Lord, thank you that every need I have this day has been met! You always come through for me! You never cease to amaze me. You are an awesome God. All glory and honor belong to you! Amen!

Day 23

"This means that anyone who belongs to Christ has become a new person. The old life is gone; a new life has begun" 2Corinthians 5:17 (NLT).

IT'S TIME TO CHANGE

As humans, we go through different stages in our lives. We go from infancy, childhood, and from adolescence to adulthood. As infants, we are dependent on others to meet our needs until we are able to do things on our own. So it is with our life as Christians. After we have been born again; go through the rebirth process, we are babes in Christ. We are dependent on others to pray for us, to counsel us, to hold our hands as we begin our journey with the Lord. Infants can only drink milk until they have developed teeth and their system can handle eating solid food. They have to be taught right from wrong until they are mature enough to know the difference and make good choices. Babes in Christ can only drink milk until they are mature enough to eat solid food. The problem is, today, there are too many babes in Christ. The Apostle Paul said, "You have been believers so long now that you ought to be teaching others. Instead, you need someone to teach you again the basic things about God's word. You are like babes who need milk and cannot eat solid food" (Hebrews 5:12).

It's time to change! It's time for those of us in the Body of Christ to allow God to make changes in our lives so we can do the work He has assigned for us to do. To not grow in Christ, means we can't go where he wants to send us.

The Lord said something to me about a person who was in my life, and I was praying for things to turn around in our relationship. This is what the Lord said to me, "Daughter, he's not willing to make the necessary changes required to go where I'm taking you!" So, I had to move on with my life. Whatever changes need to be made in your life, let God get to the root of the matter and set you free. In order for us to move forward in God, we have to let him deal with those issues that will hinder our growth. Change is hard, but God is a healer. Decide today if you want to change. Ask the Lord to help you be a better husband/wife, a better father/mother, or a better son/daughter. Ask him to help you have the right attitude, to walk in love, to be a better employee on your job, to be a better student in school. When you ask, you shall receive! Let him take you through the process and transform you into the mature Christian Paul speaks about in the word. No more milk!

Lord, I submit my will to your will so that you can make the necessary changes in me and then I can be used for your glory. In Jesus' name, amen!

Day 24

"Then said Jesus unto his disciples, If any man will come after me, let him deny himself, and take up his cross, and follow me" (Matthew 16:24).

FOLLOW ME!

My pastor, Apostle Kidd, tells us the Lord has him put aside the sermon on some Sundays and says, "Follow Me." I had this happen to me on several occasions. God instructed me to follow him. I believe one reason is to show us that we can depend on God to use us any way he chooses. Whether it's with a prepared sermon/teaching or not. Two, it teaches us when we obey God and trust him to deliver, he will! It builds our faith in God and reminds us that we are nothing and can do nothing without him! In Matthew 4:18-19, Jesus was walking by the sea of Galilee when he saw two brothers, Simon Peter and Andrew. These two brothers were fishermen, Jesus told them to "Follow me and I will make you fishers of men." These two brothers, along with the other men Jesus told to follow him, became His disciples. They took a step of faith and left what they had: businesses, their homes and families to partner with Jesus to win souls for the Kingdom. What are you willing to give up to follow Jesus? Are you willing to leave the comforts of this life to follow him?

When I moved to Atlanta in July of 2000, I left my cushiony job, taking a huge cut in pay. Before moving to Atlanta, the Lord had me to make a move that really took courage for me and that was to leave my home church. That was the church I grew up in. I knew just about everyone there. My family was a part of this church, but the Lord spoke to me and said, "I want you to go to the ABC Church, (I won't reveal the real name)." I went. That was God's plan before the foundation of the world for me! He was teaching me how to walk by faith. Now, in doing so, I was talked about. My family didn't understand what was going on with me, but God was taking me on a journey with him, and I was and still am learning to trust him. I'm learning more about him through fellowshipping with him and spending time in His presence. Following Jesus requires we forget about our will and way and let him take charge of our lives. Go where He sends us and know that where he guides he also provides. There have been some trials and hard aches, but God has always brought me through. I wouldn't trade this life with Jesus for anything in the world! He is the best thing that has ever happened to me! And following him, I have no regrets! There is a song I sang in the choir at the church where I grew up. It is called "I Have Decided to Follow Jesus." I still sing that song today. The words say, "I have decided to follow Jesus, I have decided to follow Jesus, I have decided to follow Jesus, no turning back! No turning back!" If you decide to follow Jesus, he'll make it worth your while.

Lord, I will follow you wherever you lead. I forget about my plans so that your perfect plan for my life will manifest. Where you guide, I believe you always provide! In the name of Jesus, amen!

$\mathcal{D}$ay 25

"Wherefore seeing we also are compassed about with so great a cloud of witnesses, let us lay aside every weight, and the sin which doth so easily beset us, and let us run with patience the race that is before us" (Hebrews 12:1).

GET RID OF THE BAGGAGE

When traveling by plane, I would put as much as I could in a carry-on luggage so I would not have to check my bags and wait to pick it up once I arrive to my destination. I wanted to get where I was going and not have to deal with any extra baggage. That's how it is in life; we have so much baggage we're carrying it hinders us from moving forward. Baggage from a bad marriage that ended in divorce. Or maybe, it's baggage we have from our youth, something that happened to us years ago that we have not released, baggage from a relationship/friendship that we need to sever ties with and sin that's weighing us down.

God does not want us weighed down with baggage. "Let us lay aside every weight, and sin which doth so easily beset us" (Hebrews 12:1b). It's time to let go of things and people in our lives that hinder our progress and spiritual growth. This could mean letting go of friends and family that may be near and dear to you. A few years ago, I remember asking the Lord to sever any relationships I have that He knows are not good for me. It wasn't long before a young lady, who I had been friends with for a few years, stopped speaking to me and begin to be distant. I asked her if there was something I did or said to

56

her that caused her to stop speaking to me. She said there wasn't anything. Then, what I asked the Lord came back to me. Now, there was nothing bad about this young lady. Eventually, she started back speaking to me, but we were going in different directions. God did just what I asked him because he knew we were going in different directions. Everybody is not going where God is taking us, so we have to learn how to let go.

Sin in our lives will also keep us from growing spiritually. I told you I was a fornicator and enjoyed having sex with men I was in a relationship with (sin is pleasurable for a season). But, after that season of pleasure, I began to get tired physically as well as spiritually. One day, I remember getting on my knees at the foot of my bed and crying out to the Lord. I confessed, "I'm tired of this way of living. I know this is not the life you have for me, and I want to do better. God, I need your help!"

"For I know that in me (that is, in my flesh,) dwelleth no good thing; for to will is present with me; but how to perform that which is good I find not" (Romans 7:18).

God answered my prayer, but I had to do my part which was not put myself in situations that would cause me to sin. Did it happen overnight? No, I slipped up many times, but God was faithful. Just like God answered my prayer, he will do the same for you. He will help you by His spirit to get rid of the baggage in your life, so you can be the godly man/woman he has called you to be.

Lord, I choose to walk by the spirit so I will not gratify the desires of the flesh. I get rid of the weight and sin that has kept me bound. I will not bring sorrow to your Holy Spirit by the way I live. I have a new life in You and the old me is dead, In Jesus' name, amen!

$\mathcal{D}$ay 26

"The effectual fervent prayer of a righteous man availeth much" (James 5:16b).

IT'S PRAYER TIME!

In the church, where I grew up in Chicago, I would often hear one of the deacons say, "Its prayer time." In other words, he was saying, it was time to pray. Man was he right. It was time to pray and it still is. Prayer is essential in the life of the believer. We cannot live and operate in this world without spending time talking to our Father and getting the instructions we need for each day. When I was younger, I would pray "Now lay me down to sleep, I pray the Lord my soul to keep, if I should die before I wake I pray the Lord my soul to take." Then I would ask the Lord to bless my parents and siblings. As I got older, I was taught in Sunday school about praying the Lord's Prayer. When I became an adult and began to learn more about the Lord, I began praying like a mature Christian. I would pray at home but not in public. That was because of the fear of not being able to pray like the other adults. I also thought praying was laborious. I felt it was taking away time for me to do things I like, such as watching my favorite television show, hanging out with my friends or other fun things. The Lord used a young lady in my life to tell me that prayer is not scripted; it's what comes from your heart. It's having a conversation with God like you would your friends. She said to start out spending five minutes with God and then each week increase my time. Well, can I be honest? I didn't do exactly what she said. For years, I struggled with being consistent in my prayer time with God. I went to Intercessory Prayer Training class at my church and even joined a prayer group. I would ask God to please help me be consistent with my prayer time. I would start out doing good, then I would get off. Then, one day something happened, and I had to trust God to help me get through that problem in my life. I would pray every day and talk to the Lord about the situation and ask him to show me what to do. Now, unfortunately something happened to get me to be serious about spending time with the Lord.

Don't let a calamity or problem happen in your life to make you spend time with the Lord. Spending time in prayer is not just for us, God wants to fellowship with us too! He gave Adam instructions for his life, Genesis 2:15-18. God and Adam fellowshipped with one another. Jesus prayed for us in John 17. We were created to fellowship with God. We can tell the Lord anything, all our secrets that he knows already, but he still wants us to talk to him, and he won't tell anyone what we shared with each other. We are at a crucial time in our society, and we need to communicate with the father. He gives us the peace we need to help us during these perilous times. We have no need to fear because God/Jesus is in control! If we want to see a change in our lives and live victoriously like God intended, we need to pray. We need to pray for our country and its leaders. We need to pray for our families, our church family, our schools, our communities, our jobs, the poor and needy. We need to pray and tear down the kingdom of darkness including pornography, sex trafficking, drug sales and drug use. We need to pray and come against gang activity, gang violence, and that murdering demon. We need to pray against racism, sexism, child abuse, spousal abuse and everything that the enemy has distorted. Its prayer time people! It's time to pray!

Lord, you said that we are to always pray. I will not give up or quit! I will seek your face and fellowship with you day and night. In the name of Jesus, amen!

$\mathcal{D}$ay 27

"But He was wounded for our transgressions, he was bruised for our iniquities: the chastisement of our peace was upon him; and with his stripes we are healed" (Isaiah 53:5 KJV).

IT'S A FIGHT, BUT WE WIN!

Recently, on social media, a friend of mine posted this comment, "Jesus healed me and I'm keeping it!" I responded to the post and said, "You betta!" I said that because, yes, Jesus has already healed us! "He personally carried our sins in his body on the cross so that we can be dead to sin and live for what is right. By his wounds you are healed" 1 Peter 2:24 (NLT). But we have to fight to keep it! We have an enemy named Satan, who will bring thoughts to our mind to say different than what the word says. He will show you a pop up menu with all the health issues that you could possibly have. You start having some symptoms or pain, and he'll show you things that could be wrong with you. He'll show you cancer, then swipe and show you heart failure. He'll swipe again to show you high blood pressure, diabetes and arthritis. He'll keep swiping until you cast those thoughts down and tell him to go in the name of Jesus! Sometimes even the people you hang around with will start to say things about you. Out of ignorance, they will say, "You know my mother had those same symptoms, and she died!" People, let me tell you when God says that you are healed get ready to fight and hold on to your healing. The enemy's job is "to steal, and to kill, and to destroy," but Jesus came so that we could have abundant life!" (John 10:10). Whatever the issue is, God, has already remedied it on the cross. We have to fight for our healing, our families, our finances, our marriage, our job, our sanity, and even our country! We fight with the word of God! When Jesus was tempted of the devil, he fought back. Not with physical weapons, but spiritual weapons, the word.

In Luke 4:1-13, Every time Satan tempted him, Jesus whipped him with the word, and he won because He (Jesus) is the winner! You and I are winners too! We must start with the word and end with the word. That's why it's important to pray and fellowship with the Father and confess the word over our lives and the life of our families every day! "Death and life are in the power of the tongue: and they that love it shall eat the fruit thereof," Proverbs 18:21. So, I ask you this question, do you want to speak life (the word of God) or death over your life? The choice is yours. Yes, it's a fight, but we already have the victory!

Lord, I will fight the good fight of faith each day! I have your word as my sword to defeat the enemy. The battle is not mine but yours, so I always win. In the name of Jesus, amen!

Day 28

"Don't copy the behavior and customs of this world, but let God transform you into a new person by changing the way you think. Then you will learn to know God's will for you, which is good and pleasing and perfect" Romans 12:2 (NLT).

CLEAN UP THE CLUTTER!

I f there's one thing I can't stand, it is clutter. I can't stand clutter in my home or in my classroom at work. The word clutter means a collection of things lying about in an untidy mass. I knew someone who had and still has a lot of clutter in their home. Let's just say their name is BB. This individual would collect things that people would throw away and keep it in their home. BB would even take empty milk cartons and other food containers, rinse them and place it in the cabinets. I know the idiom "One man's trash is another man's treasure," but there is something wrong when that treasure is just being collected and not being used for any good. I didn't understand why BB was comfortable with all this clutter in their home. The Lord showed me that the problem is in their mind. They have a poverty mentality. This person confessed Christ as their Lord and Savior, but their mind has to be renewed. In Ephesians 4:17-32, the Apostle Paul teaches us to not live like the Gentiles or sinners, but "Instead, let the Spirit renew your thoughts and attitude," Ephesians 4:23 (NLT). My former pastor would tell us "You can take the person out of the ghetto, but you can't get the ghetto out of the person." I understand what he meant by that statement.

Because BB wasn't filling their mind and heart with the word of God, the physical clutter was only a reflection of what was in their mind. BB was sitting up under the word of God every Sunday but not putting into practice what he had learned from hearing the word.

What's cluttering your mind? Do you have a poverty mentality? Do you want more money to pile into your savings and IRA accounts to have all to yourself? Do you work and work so you can get more money but have a hard time giving to someone in need, or even enjoying what you worked for? Are you piling up more and more, thinking if you don't, you will lose it all? You need to be set free in your mind! Jesus wants us to be made whole in our spirit, soul, (mind, will, and emotions) and body. Don't let the clutter in your mind cause you to miss out on what God has for you. Get rid of the clutter in your mind so you can see and receive what the Lord has for you. Get rid of the clutter in your mind so you can hear him speak to you. Clean up the clutter so you can live the life he has predestined you to live!

"Lord Jesus, help me by your Spirit to get rid of the clutter in my mind! Help me through your word to clear my mind of old habits and ungodly thinking. I speak to my mind, no more clutter in the name of Jesus! I have the mind of Christ and the wisdom of God is formed within me! I am free from bondage and stinking thinking! Whom the son set free is free indeed, and since I belong to you (Jesus), I am free in my spirit and mind. I no longer think like the world nor do I copy the world's attitude and behavior; their way of living and being right, but I copy the behavior of Jesus. I talk like him, love like him, and pattern my life after Jesus! I am a new person, the old me is gone, and the new me has begun. I choose to think on things that are pure, true, just, honest, lovely, and praiseworthy. I am the redeemed of the Lord, and I'm saying so. I thank you Lord for what you have done in me, in Jesus' name, amen!"

$\mathcal{D}$ay 29

"O give thanks unto the LORD; for he is good: because his mercy endureth forever"

(Psalm 118:1)

THANK YOU!

As a child, I was taught to always say thank you when someone did or said something nice. I taught my sons to do the same thing, and they have taught their children as well. One day, while sitting in my loft, I began to sing this song titled "Thank You Lord." The words thank you just kept coming out of my mouth. I began to think about God's goodness and mercy, and I just broke out singing this song. I thought about how the Lord saved my soul, how he used people in my life to lead me to Him. That in itself is amazing to me. God chose me to be a part of his royal family before the foundation of the world. He knew the day and the hour I would cry out to him for help. Then, I thought about that day and the fact that I have a living mother, I have a beautiful family, I can breathe on my own, walk on my own and feed myself. I have clothes and shoes and a place that I can call home, all the things we sometime forget to say thank you for on a daily basis. Our saying "thank you" to the Lord each morning shows our gratitude and appreciation to him.

Psalm 107:1-2 **"O give thanks unto the LORD, for he is good: for his mercy endureth forever. Let the redeemed of the LORD say so, whom he hath redeemed from the hand of the enemy."**

Since we are the redeemed of the Lord, we should say "Thank you Lord!" Thank God during the good times, the hard times, during trials, test, and temptations. Thank God for little things like a good parking space, a good grade on an exam, for favor with your boss or teacher. Thank the Lord for good weather, the sunshine, and for leading you to the right store and purchasing the item you want at the price you want. Thank him when things are not going the way you want and trust him to see you through. Those things may seem small but those are signs of God's presence. That's Him letting us know that he cares about everything that concerns us. Thank God for everything he has done already that has manifested and those things that have yet to manifest. Thank him for his faithfulness, his mercy, his kindness, his everlasting love, his healing power, saving power, provision and for just being who he is! He is God almighty, the omnipresent one, omnipotent God, sovereign God! He's the great I AM God, the Holy one, righteous God, a just God, our protector, friend, deliverer and lover of our soul! He's God! There is no one greater! If God were to never do anything else, all that he has done we can tell him thank you! We are to always have a heart of gratitude and thankfulness every day throughout the day! Don't let a day go by without thanking God! Just say "Thank you!"

Lord, thank you for redeeming my life from the enemy. Thank you for new mercies this day! As long as there is breath in me, I will praise you and give you thanks. Amen!

$\mathcal{D}$ay 30

Ask, and it shall be given you; seek and ye shall find; knock, and it shall be opened unto you" (Matthew 7:7)

<u>JESUS IS THE ANSWER!</u>

No matter what happens in your life, Jesus is the answer! Whatever problem you're facing or whatever the situation may be, Jesus is the answer. We sang a song back in the day at the church I grew up in titled "Jesus Is the Answer." I realized how true that song was one day. I was looking for a dress to wear to a dinner dance fundraiser I was to attend for my job. I was frustrated because it was close to the day of the event, and I still didn't have a dress to wear. I had looked and looked in different stores and could not find a dress that fit me right. I called my friend and asked her if she would go with me to look for a dress in the mall. I had gone to every store where I thought I would be able to get the dress but hadn't gone to the mall near my house. She agreed and she went with me.

Now, this was at a time in my life where I was learning how to pray and ask God for anything. So, we're at the mall and we went from store to store. I still could not find what I was looking for. Then my friend said, "Lord, I thank you that you will lead us to the right store so we can find the right dress for Janice to wear to the event in Jesus name, amen!" She was praying as we were walking through the mall. We went up to the second level of the mall. Low and behold, we see a store called The Answer. My friend said, "The answer, the answer. Well, Jesus is the answer!" We laughed, went inside, and the Lord lead us to the right dress. The dress was beautiful, and it was a perfect fit!

"You can ask any thing in my name, and I will do it, so that the Son can bring glory to the Father. Yes, ask me for anything in my name, and I will do it!" John 14:13-14(NLT).

Jesus was the answer, He said yes, and the answer was a store named "The answer!" How about that? She prayed and asked in Jesus name and He answered with leading us to the right store, with the right dress and the right price. Now, that was the first time I heard someone pray like that. So, you know what? That taught me I can ask God for anything, and he will give it to me. My asking God for anything must be anything that's legal! I don't want anyone to think they can ask God for things that are illegal, unethical, or immoral and think he will grant it. Nope! It's not going to happen like that! The word says, **"And we are confident that he hears us whenever we ask for anything that <u>pleases him</u>, and since we know he hears us, when we make our requests, we also know that he will give us what we ask for"** 1 **John 5:14-15 (NLT).** The key words in that verse are **"anything that pleases him."** The dress I needed was not for God but for me. But it pleased him because it is his will to see that I have whatever I need when I need it! Just like Jesus answered our prayer that day for something simple as a dress, you can believe that he will answer your prayer. Getting Jesus involved in our situations takes the pressure off us and makes things go smoothly. When we get him involved in everything we do (all our plans, our dreams, and our goals), he will, by his Spirit, guide us in the right direction! Get Jesus involved! Ask him each morning to guide you throughout the day, to help you make the right decisions, so you won't stumble and fall. When we get in his presence each day, he will give us what we need to get through the day. The answers to the questions we have are in him. Jesus is the answer!

Lord, God thank you that answers are waiting for me in your presence. Everything I need is in you! I have confidence in you that when I pray according to your will you have heard me and granted my petitions. In Jesus' name, amen!

Day 31

"Get rid of all bitterness, rage, anger, harsh words, and slander; as well as all types of evil behavior. Instead, be kind to each other; tenderhearted, forgiving one another; just as God through Christ has forgiven you" (Ephesians 4:31-32).

FORGIVE SO YOU CAN BE HEALED!

"And forgive us our sins, as we have forgiven those who sin against us" Matthew 6:12 (NLT). In this chapter of Matthew the Lord Jesus is teaching us how to pray. This part of the prayer says that we are to forgive others just like we want God to forgive us. How many times have we prayed the Lord's Prayer and really thought about forgiving others of their sins against us? We want the Lord to forgive us of our sins, but do we really forgive others? We see it every day in the world. When someone commits a sin against us, we want that person to be punished, and depending on the sin and who committed it, we want that person to suffer and God to get them good!

Peter, one of Jesus' disciples, asked, "How many times should I forgive someone who sins against me, 'Till seven times?'" Jesus replied, "Until seventy times seven!" Jesus wasn't giving him a set number of times but an endless number of times of how we should forgive. My ex-husband abused me emotionally, and after we divorced, I realized later, I had bitterness and unforgiveness in my heart towards him. We attended the same church and I would speak to him when I saw him, but I really had bitterness in my heart towards him. I would think about the times he had said or done something that was hurtful and disrespectful to me. Things that he never apologized for. One Sunday after church, I was talking to a friend of mine about an incident that happened at work. She looked at me and told me a story about a young lady who had a similar situation and said to me, "You are angry about something or someone, and you need to ask the Lord to show you what it is and deal with it! Because if you don't deal with it now you'll deal with it later and it will hinder the plan of God for your life." When she said that, I knew it was the Holy Spirit speaking through her to me. Yes, I had to deal with that anger, and I did! I went to the Lord and asked him to show me where was this coming from. Show me why am I behaving like this?

The Lord is so merciful and gracious, and He is the Healer. He showed me the anger was coming from a root of bitterness and unforgiveness towards my ex-husband because of the way he treated me. I asked the Lord to help me because I knew that was not the character of God. I asked him to help me forgive him and love him with the love of Jesus. I had to forgive him! I had to forgive him so I could be healed! I had to forgive him so God could use me to write this devotional! It had nothing to do with my ex. I'm sure he had moved on, but I needed to be free of the pain and past hurt. My pastor, Apostle Kidd, taught on forgiveness some years ago. He said, "There are three components of forgiveness. Forgiveness must have **TIMING**." Acts 7:59-60 (NLT), "As they stoned him, Stephen prayed, "Lord Jesus, receive my spirit." He fell to his knees shouting, "Lord, don't charge them with this sin!" And with that, he died." We must forgive the person before the sin is committed. While the sin is being committed, and after they've sinned against us, forgiveness must have **TRACTION**! It must have stick-to-itiveness! We must have resolved in our mind that we will forgive just like Jesus forgave us. Forgiveness must have **TOTALITY**! It requires that we forgive the person or persons who wronged us one hundred percent and forget what was said or done, never bringing it up ever again! "As far as the east is from the west, so far hath he removed our transgressions from us" (Psalm 103:12).

God does not bring up our sins to taunt us or remind us of how we messed up. That's what Satan does; he continues to remind us of our past sins and what others have done to us. He does it so that we will miss what God has for us and so that root of bitterness will manifest in us, our children, and our children's children until we say "enough is enough!" and do it Loves way! When Satan attacks us in our mind, we have the word of God to fight with. "Casting down imaginations, and every high thing that exalteth itself against the knowledge of God; bringing into captivity every thought to the obedience of Christ" (2Corinthians 10:5). We are to forgive others like Jesus forgave us. Even now, He continues to forgive us when we mess up. If you're struggling with unforgiveness, I encourage you to let Jesus minister to you through his word. Don't let a root of bitterness grow into anger, resentment, and hatred. It will prevent you from being healed physically and spiritually. The Lord can't bless us nor will he hear our prayers with unforgiveness in our heart. Whatever it is, let it go! Forgive and let Jesus heal you!

Lord Jesus, your word says that you have forgiven me of my sins and trespasses, so, therefore as you have forgiven me, I also forgive others who have sinned and trespassed against me. I uproot any bitterness, anger, and hatred in my heart against those who have sinned against me in the past, present, and future. I replace it with happiness, joy, and love. I choose to walk in love because you are love and it is the more excellent way to live. I thank you for your Holy Spirit working in and through me to walk in love, forgive, and to forget those things that are in my past and look forward to what lies ahead. Lord, I can do nothing without you, but I can do all things through you, who gives me strength! I thank you, Lord, for what you have already done in me. In Jesus' name! Amen!

God Loves Me Too!

Confessing God's word over our lives and our family is a powerful thing. "Death and life are in the power of the tongue, and they that love it shall eat the fruit thereof" (Proverbs 18:22).

I believe as you confess what God's word says about you, your health, your finances, marriage, family, business and more, you will begin to see change in your life. Your way of thinking will change, and you will see yourself and your situation the way God sees it. The first and most important confession we should make is to receive Jesus as our Lord and Savior. If you have not done so already, I encourage you to do so today. Why put off for tomorrow, what you can do today because tomorrow isn't promised to any of us! 1 Corinthians 15:3-4 is the Gospel of Jesus Christ! He died for our sins, was buried, and rose again. Now, if you believe that, then Romans 10:9, 10, & 13 says, "That if thou will confess with thy mouth the Lord Jesus and believe in your heart that God has raised him from the dead, you shall be saved. For with the heart man believes unto righteousness, and with the mouth confession is made known unto salvation. For whosoever shall call on the name of the Lord shall be saved." With that in mind, repeat this prayer after me:

Heavenly Father, I confess to you I have sinned, but I ask you Lord to forgive me for all of my sins. I accept Jesus as my Lord and Savior, and I ask him to come into my heart right now and save my soul, give me eternal life, and baptize me with The Holy Ghost. In Jesus' name I pray and give thanks, Amen.

If you have prayed this prayer sincerely with all your heart, then you are saved. Immediately the Spirit of God comes into your heart and lives in you. You are now born again by the blood of Jesus. If you don't have a church home, ask the Lord to lead you by his spirit to where He wants you to be spiritually fed. Be faithful to the Lord by attending the church where he plants you regularly and allow him to use the man or woman of God to minister to you so you can grow in the Lord. I pray God's blessings upon you and your loved ones! I love you with the love of the Lord!

Your sister-in-Christ,

Janice

About the Author

Janice is the daughter of Carrie Robinson and the late Charles Robinson, the mother of two sons and grandmother of eleven. She grew up on the westside of Chicago, but currently resides in Georgia and is a member of Destiny Christian Center Church International in Lithonia, Georgia where Apostle Julius H. Kidd is pastor and teacher.

Janice received her calling into the ministry in 2004 and was trained under the tutelage of Apostle Kidd. She is an ordained minister of the gospel and the Lord has placed the mantle of evangelism on her life. As a former school teacher, Janice has a love for helping children and young women. God uses her to share her testimony with many and to encourage them to be all that God created them to be.